WITHDRAWN

I LIKE
GREAT DANES!

Linda Bozzo

It is the Mission of the American Canine Association (ACA) to provide registered dog owners with the educational support needed for raising, training, showing, and breeding the healthiest pets expected by responsible pet owners throughout the world. Through our activities and services, we encourage and support the dog world in order to promote best-known husbandry standards as well as to ensure that the voice and needs of our customers are quickly and properly addressed.

Our continued support, commitment, and direction are guided by our customers, including veterinary, legal, and legislative advisors. ACA aims to provide the most efficient, cooperative, and courteous service to our customers and strives to set the standard for education and problem solving for all who depend on our services.

For more information, please visit www.acacanines.com, e-mail customerservice@acadogs.com, phone 1-800-651-8332, or write to the American Canine Association at PO Box 121107, Clermont, FL 34712.

Published in 2017 by Enslow Publishing, LLC.
101 W. 23rd Street, Suite 240, New York, NY 10011

Library of Congress Cataloging-in-Publication Data
Names: Bozzo, Linda.
Title: I like great danes! / Linda Bozzo.
Description: New York : Enslow Publishing, 2017 | Series: Discover dogs with the American Canine Association | Includes bibliographical references and index. | Audience: Ages 5 and up. | Audience: Grades K to 3.
Identifiers: ISBN 978-0-7660-7781-2 (library bound) | ISBN 978-0-7660-7792-8 (pbk.) | ISBN 978-0-7660-7764-5 (6 pack)
Subjects: LCSH: Great Dane--Juvenile literature. | Dogs--Juvenile literature.
Classification: LCC SF429.G7 B69 2017 | DDC 636.73--dc23

Printed in Malaysia

To Our Readers: We have done our best to make sure all website addresses in this book were active and appropriate when we went to press. However, the author and the publisher have no control over and assume no liability for the material available on those websites or on any websites they may link to. Any comments or suggestions can be sent by e-mail to customerservice@enslow.com.

Photo Credits: Cover, p. 1 Eric Isselee/Shutterstock.com; p. 3 belu gheorghe/Shutterstock.com (left), juza/Shutterstock.com (right); p. 4 Elsa Hoffmann/Shutterstock.com; p. 5 Dmussmann/Shutterstock.com; p. 6 Juza/Shutterstock.com; p. 7 Victoria Rak/Shutterstock.com; p. 8 Mel Yates/Taxi/Getty Images; p. 9 Siri Stafford/Thinkstock; p. 10 everydoghasastory/Shutterstock.com; p. 11 Guy J. Sagi/Shutterstock.com; p. 13 Lauren Burke/Stone/Getty Images (great dane eating), jclegg/shutterstock.com (collar), Luisa Leal Photography (bed), gvictoria/Shutterstock.com (brush), In-Finity/Shutterstock.com (dishes), iStock.com/Lisa Thornberg (leash, toys); p. 14 Ron Chappie Stock/Thinkstock; p. 14 iStock.com/Chris Bernard Photography; p. 15 Tannis Toohey/Toronto Star/Getty Images; p. 16 TIMOTHY A. CLARY/AFP/Getty Images; p. 17; Anna Hoychuk/Shutterstock.com (top), © Pictorial Press Ltd/Alamy Stock Photo (Scooby); p. 18 iStock.com/Chris Bernard Photography, Inc; p. 19 Marcel Jancovic/Shutterstock.com; p. 21 Dina Rudick/The Boston Globe via Getty Image; p. 22 Annette Shaff/Shutterstock.com.

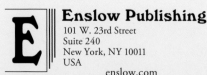

Enslow Publishing
101 W. 23rd Street
Suite 240
New York, NY 10011
USA
enslow.com

CONTENTS

IS A GREAT DANE RIGHT FOR YOU?

Great Danes are friendly with other pets and great with children. They need lots of space, so large homes are best for this very large breed.

Great Danes are one of the largest breeds of dogs.

A DOG OR A PUPPY?

Young Great Dane puppies are cute and small. They grow quickly into very large dogs. Early training is best due to their large size. If you do not have time to train a puppy, an older Great Dane may be better for your family.

LOVING YOUR GREAT DANE

Take good care of your Great Dane. Cuddle with him. Play with him. Great Danes are easy to love!

FAST FACT:
Great Danes are known as gentle giants.

EXERCISE

Great Danes enjoy playing games like **fetch** in large spaces. Walks on a **leash** will help to stretch their long legs.

It takes a while for the bones and joints of these large dogs to stop growing and become stable. Your Great Dane puppy should have limited exercise until he's at least 18 months old.

FEEDING YOUR GREAT DANE

Great Danes need to be fed a special diet due to their large size. This breed needs to rest shortly after eating.

Ask a **veterinarian** (vet), a doctor for animals, which food is best for your large-breed dog and how much to feed her.

Give your Great Dane fresh, clean water every day.

Remember to keep your dog's food and water dishes clean. Dirty dishes can make a dog sick.

Do not feed your dog people food.
It can make her sick.

Your new dog will need:

a collar with a tag

a bed

a brush

food and water dishes

a leash

toys

GROOMING

Great Danes **shed**. This means their short smooth hair falls out. They should be bathed and brushed as needed. Because of their large size, bathing Great Danes can be hard.

A Great Dane's nails will need to be clipped. A vet or **groomer** can show you how. Your dog's ears should be cleaned, and his teeth should be brushed by an adult.

WHAT YOU SHOULD KNOW

Great Danes are friendly and gentle.

They are calm in the house.

These dogs don't bark much but make good watchdogs because of their size.

Because of their large size and strength, Great Danes need to be watched around small children. They can accidentally knock them over.

FUN FACT:
The famous cartoon character Scooby-Doo was a Great Dane.

You will need to take your new dog to the vet for a checkup. He will need shots, called vaccinations, and yearly checkups to keep him healthy. If you think your dog may be sick, call your vet.

A GOOD FRIEND

Great Danes live up to 10 years. During that time they are great friends who will take up a large space in your heart.

NOTE TO PARENTS

It is important to consider having your dog spayed or neutered when the dog is young. Spaying and neutering are operations that prevent unwanted puppies and can help improve the overall health of your dog.

It is also a good idea to microchip your dog, in case he or she gets lost. A vet will implant a painless microchip under the skin, which can then be scanned at a vet's office or animal shelter to look up your information on a national database.

Some towns require licenses for dogs, so be sure to check with your town clerk.

For more information, speak with a vet.

There are many dogs, young and old, waiting to be adopted from animal shelters and rescue groups.

fetch – To go after a toy and bring it back.

groomer – A person who bathes and brushes dogs.

leash – A chain or strap that attaches to the dog's collar.

shed – When dog hair falls out so new hair can grow.

vaccinations – Shots that dogs need to stay healthy.

veterinarian (vet) – A doctor for animals.

Books

Johnson, Jinny. *Great Dane.* Mankato, MN: Smart Apple Media, 2015.

Person, Stephen, *Great Dane: Gentle Giant.* New York, NY: Bearport Publishing, 2012.

Rajczak, Kristen. *Great Danes.* New York, NY: Gareth Stevens Publishing, 2012.

Websites

American Canine Association Inc., Kids Corner
acakids.com/

National Geographic for Kids, Pet Central
kids.nationalgeographic.com/explore/pet-central/

PBS Kids, Dog Games
pbskids.org/games/dog/

INDEX